Perfect
Marketing

Perfect Marketing

ALL YOU NEED
TO GET IT RIGHT
FIRST TIME

LOUELLA MILES

ARROW
BUSINESS BOOKS

Published by Arrow Books in 1995

1 3 5 7 9 10 8 6 4 2

© Louella Miles 1995

First published by
Arrow Books Limited
20 Vauxhall Bridge Road, London SW1V 2SA

Random House Australia (Pty) Limited
20 Alfred Street, Milsons Point, Sydney
New South Wales 2061, Australia

Random House New Zealand Limited
18 Poland Road, Glenfield
Auckland 10, New Zealand

Random House South Africa (Pty) Limited
PO Box 337, Bergvlei, South Africa

Random House UK Limited Reg. No. 954009

ISBN 0 09 950521 5

Set in Bembo by
SX Composing Ltd, Rayleigh, Essex
Printed and bound in Great Britain by
Cox and Wyman Ltd, Reading, Berks

British Library Cataloguing in Publication Data
A catalogue record for this book is available from
the British Library

CONTENTS

INTRODUCTION

The growth of a US import. We're talking marketing – not sales

Marketing has crept up on the British public over the years. Most people would be hard put to provide a definition, hardly surprising since the discipline has changed and remains fluid.

Yet what are its origins? Has it always been here, or is it just that nobody's bothered to put a name to it?

It would be naive to say that Britain has ignored marketing, yet there are other countries, notably the US, which have given it a higher profile and devoted bigger bucks to its growth.

Back in the 1960s, American experts like Philip Kotler took the lead in defining marketing, explaining to companies that they needed to examine what their customers wanted instead of what they wanted to give them.

It is a concept easy to take on board in times of growth, less so in the midst of recession. In this decade a look at some of the best-known names, the Coca-Colas and the IBMs, highlights the danger of taking a brand – and an audience – for granted.

A Canadian firm called Cott emerged from anonymity to manufacture a variety of unbranded colas which hit both Coke and Pepsi where it hurt. If the public perceive little difference in quality in a range of products, it stands to reason they will go for the cheapest.

Marketing now has to come to grips with the whole issue of brands. The big names will survive, of course, but the question that has to be asked more frequently by owners is does the consumer still want or need its pro-duct?

IBM, meanwhile, took a knock when cheap clone makers turned personal computers into a commodity. It had to reassess the type of marketing strategy needed to meet the new challenges, namely millions of smaller customers and tens of thousands of competitors.

Cultural differences affect perceptions, too. Across the Atlantic, firms place great emphasis on sales, which though it forms part of the marketing discipline is not intended to replace it. In Europe, we talk occasionally of marketing and advertising as one and the same, even though the latter is just one element of marketing.

It is this sort of confusion that alarms the experts. At the 1994 annual conference of the Chartered Institute of Marketing, Professor Malcolm McDonald, professor of marketing planning at Cranfield School of Manage-ment, referred to one computer company that described its sales managers as marketing managers 'to give the impression that they were listening to their customers' needs'.

Consumers cannot be treated as fools. True marketing has to involve researching their needs and meeting them innovatively and cost-effectively. The alternative is not worth thinking about.

WHAT IS MARKETING?

A dying discipline or one that is more vital than ever?

WHAT IS IT?

The Chartered Institute of Marketing's definition is 'Marketing is the management process responsible for identifying, anticipating and satisfying customer requirements profitably.' Too often, though, companies pay lip service to such definitions, boasting of marketing departments whose role may be many steps removed from true marketing.

Snapshot in time

Just when it looked as though marketing was gaining credence as an essential part of a company's formula for growth, some of the biggest firms declare that they are disbanding their marketing departments. It has led to charges that marketing is facing a mid-life crisis.

So what is the true situation? If research from Cranfield School of Management, commissioned by the Chartered Institute of Marketing, is to be believed such charges are too simplistic. It concludes that in reality marketers from fast-moving consumer goods (FMCG) companies, and those in the industrial and service sectors are at different stages of evolution.

This is hardly surprising. They have been subject to different pressures, to different growth patterns, to the effects of differing technological advances. It would defy any evolutionary pattern if their respective marketing development were in step.

What price a marketing department?

Having a marketing team does not make a company immune to claims that it doesn't practise sound marketing. In practice, in the current climate, this is less likely but only because of a little thing called 'accountability'.

It is no longer a case of throwing money at a project and expecting a solution. Every penny has to be accounted for.

'Then there was the bank which recruited two hundred consumer goods marketers to get the "best marketing department in the world". But it had no idea what its source of differential advantage was. And if you ask whether customers can find a bank open, you get an even more distraught answer.'

Malcolm McDonald, Professor of marketing planning at Cranfield School of Management, at CIM 1994 conference

---

THE FUTURE

The news that companies are disbanding marketing departments is not as dire as it seems. In effect, what is happening is that organizations are restructuring in today's more competitive environment and that central marketing departments are being streamlined as a result. A side effect is that it has also prompted a greater use of outsourcing, which needs to be kept under control if it is to contribute to successful marketing.

So where is marketing taking place? More and more frequently it's occurring closer to the customers, with those staff in direct contact taking charge. It makes more sense than having a head of department, with several layers of staff between him and the end user, deciding what offer to make on which day.

This is only one side of the equation, however. Information also needs to filter in from sales and a variety of other sources to allow marketing at a strategic level to take place. It requires a constant flow of data on the marketplace, a company and its rivals, and the customers they serve. But today's marketers have a distinct advantage over their predecessors. They can practise database marketing.

DATABASE MARKETING

Faced with these two words, take a deep breath. You are not going to be blinded with science, or bombarded with jargon. Instead I hope to offer a small steer in the right direction.

Don't confuse direct marketing, which is a promotional activity, a tool, with database marketing. The only potential area of commonality is that direct marketing may use a database.

Look instead at database marketing as a new way of marketing, involving **segments**. It enables companies to understand their customers better and break them down into groupings which are easier to communicate with. It also helps them look at information on price and markets so that they can react quickly to market changes and yet still plan for future growth.

The easiest way to look at database marketing is to regard it as a three-step process:

First, you analyse the data you have available to understand your customer. In industry terms, you profile him or her, building up a picture of age, class, spending power, and the like.

Second, once you understand the profile, you move on to segment the information into manageable chunks. You can group customers by business data or demographic data, by geography or by purchasing behaviour data.

Segmentation means marketers can target campaigns more cost-effectively to those segments. You can provide different offers to different segments. It aids analysis of promotional spend per customer and response rate, and the measurement of market share and penetration.

This is because segments have one definite advantage over looking at customers individually: they tend not to change over time, it's the customers, potential and existing, who move on.

Finally, with the results to hand, you have two choices. You can, if suitable, run a promotional campaign or you can database market.

A commitment to **database market** means that all future marketing activity will revolve around the knowledge of what you have created on the database. It means you can develop a pricing strategy for each of those segments, a sales strategy, a promotional strategy, etc.

The process of database marketing feeds itself, turning into a continuous loop. Information will come in to reinforce strategies or suggest new ones. Later on, two forms of marketing will be discussed: top down and bottom up. Database marketing is a true form of bottom up, where information from customers can be used to plan future strategy.

Step by step guide

As in any marketing activity, the first need is to define your business objectives. The next is to ensure that the database fits them. You need to know what each of your customer groupings wants and then provide them with the products or services to match. You hope to promote the benefits successfully, and measure target market penetration. Database marketing is the key.

First, define those objectives

Second, work out the data needed to achieve them

Third, evaluate the data available, internally and externally

Fourth, set the standards this data have to meet (extent of information, how up to date is it?)

Fifth, work out how you're going to improve what you've got.

Promotional back-up

How can database marketing help with a campaign? The answer is, on a number of fronts. It can assist at the beginning in defining the copy to be used and its tone for each segment. It can select who it should be aimed at, it can run a direct marketing campaign, it can monitor costs of above and below the line promotions, recording responses to it and sales. And finally, when it is over, it can analyse the campaign and generate leads.

Sales salvo

As many drugs companies have learnt, database marketing can sharpen the effectiveness of costly sales teams by monitoring their work and showing gaps or overmanning. Used properly it can also build up a picture of the whole market, measure the performance of a company's products against those of its rivals and monitor attitudes to its brands.

External pressures

Database marketing is probably the most valuable tool in a marketer's armoury. For while consumers may, in some respects, have never had it so good in terms of product choice and competitive pricing, retailers and suppliers are under greater pressure than ever. Slimmer margins, high advertising costs, reduced budgets for innovation, streamlined workforces, all squeeze a marketer's room for manoeuvre.

It is a fight to get a product on shelf, a fight to keep it there, and a fight to retain or increase customer share. All is determined by a marketer's proficiency in predicting and satisfying consumers' demands cost-effectively and the ability to negotiate successfully with retailers.

The buzzword of the 1990s has been segmentation. It has come about with the realization that the days of mass marketing are over. If television can no longer deliver in bulk, it is up to brand owners to segment their audiences so that they can target more effectively.

FIT TO MARKET

A marketing approach which works one year is never guaranteed to work the next or the one after. The big international companies have learnt this to their cost. The key is to hit on the right one for the right time.

'In the 60s and 70s all IBM had to say was "here's the product; this is the price; get in the queue." Marketing then was about managing relationships with IBM's board-level customers.'

Mike Mawtus, marketing director of IBM UK at CIM conference 1994

The challenge for IBM UK in the 1980s was to develop a marketing strategy which met the needs of a burgeoning marketplace and a myriad of competitors. Its answer was one which proved particularly attractive in the high-tech market: it linked up with a number of business partners, each with their own customers and markets, to make it more responsive and versatile.

It underlines the one constant in marketing: the need to understand customer needs and problems and for the whole company to be responsive to those needs.

SERVE THE CUSTOMER

It can't be repeated too often. Whatever the sector, marketers should aim for one common goal, serving the customer, both internal and external. It is a pursuit which will require every weapon in the marketing armoury: a committed board, a far-sighted strategy, planning acumen and market research to anticipate customer needs.

The time is right for such an approach. The UK, despite the Government's Charter Initiatives, still has some way to go in raising service standards. Consumers also have higher expectations than they used to. There is another problem, too. We have a reputation for being a nation of cynics.

So what will it take to instigate change? Money, for one thing. It costs ten times as much to win new customers as to retain old ones. Loyalty is one of the fastest growing areas of consumer marketing. The bad news is that consumers are much less loyal nowadays. They can even be called promiscuous. There needs to be recognition, too, that the public is not so easily fooled by lip service to customer service, let alone to environmental, community, or quality issues.

Lessons from the US
Retailers' attitudes to consumers in the UK have changed, but maybe it's time for a quick glimpse at the best of what the US has to offer.

Take the world's largest dairy store, Stew Leonard's in the US.[1] It achieves sales of $2,974 per square foot, exceeding that of Marks and Spencer's flagship Marble Arch store. Yet it carries only 800 products, compared with a US supermarket store average of 15,000.

Its success, it appears, is based on its customer policy. It may use the latest computer technology to ensure the smooth running of the store, the produce may be always fresh, its pricing strategy competitive, yet it is its slavish devotion to customers that ensures its performance. At Stew Leonard's, when they say the customer is always right, they mean it.

1 Taken from Manchester Business School report, *The Service Route to Profits*, produced in association with Cadogan Management.

How many retailers, hand on heart, can claim the same in the UK? The world of marketing is having to do a spot of navel gazing at the moment – and not before time.

2
MARKETING PLANNING

Organizing for effective marketing (the essential 'p's)

The previous chapter described the need to focus on the customer, be they consumer or client, internal or external. But to do this requires an understanding of what they want, how this relates to your organization, the market and whether or not you can deliver. Indeed, do you even want to deliver?

It took the harsh realities of a recession to make marketers take a long hard look at the content and cost of marketing activities and the likely return on investment. For too long the old saying, 'I know 50 per cent of my advertising works: I just don't know which half' had been taken at face value. Now the budgets just aren't there to throw behind projects.

So maybe the first thing to do is sit back and take stock. What, as a general rule, does a marketer have to contend with? These elements are often described, somewhat simplistically, as the four 'P's: product, price, place and promotion.

An existing product – or service – may be worth a mini audit to determine what influences purchasing decisions:

Product   Packaging
Positioning
Pertinence
Lifestyle appeal
Branding
Range
Size
Service promise
Reputation
Warranty

Price	Premium
	Cut price
	Flexible
	Seasonal
	Wholesale/Retail
	Added value
Place	Retail
	Direct
	Cash and Carry
	Trade marketing
	On-shelf position
Promotion	Advertising
	Sales promotion
	Direct marketing
	Merchandising
	Public relations
	Sponsorship

This list is geared more to product than service marketing, but the essentials are the same. It is up to the marketer to rank them in order of priority according to what the customer wants and what the company can afford. The other element which should not be ignored is distribution channels, an increasingly important factor, which need to be monitored to ensure cost efficiency. The growing practice of database marketing has meant more effective monitoring.

The list above is the starting point – it relates to a current situation – but it is insufficient for a marketer wishing to progress his brand. This is where the need for a marketing plan arises. It is likely to comprise the following components, and its preparation in terms of study and appraisal is likely to prove as rewarding as the end result:

corporate mission statement
financial data, past and projected
market background
marketing audit
marketing strategy
implementation programme
budgets and contingencies

When you have put together your plan, how should it be used? The danger is in viewing it as a tome to be put on the bookshelf and forgotten. It should be used as a day-to-day control and development programme.

After all, in what strategic framework are you operating? The corporate mission statement may include specific goals, such as market leadership, along with others less specific such as excellence and value for money – but are these compatible with the development of a marketing strategy whose main component has to be the desire to increase profit?

FLYING SOLO
There is another factor, too, missing from the above list. Might it make more sense to look at a strategic alliance? After all, if a company wishes to achieve critical mass yet does not wish to water down its key attributes this may be the route to success.

Look at the joint ventures in the motor and airline industries, and at the links in the pharmaceutical sector between Roche and Aspro Nicholas and Genotech. An alliance is never easy, with two different company cultures trying to work together, and it requires common goals and an element of trust, but the rewards are there for the taking.

The most attractive are cost reductions in terms of marketing and promotion, and a pooling of resources, money and personnel, in research and development. Partnerships also lead to the ability to compete more effectively on a global basis.

CORPORATE MISSION STATEMENT
This is a definition of company attributes and objectives. What is your key business activity? Along with the mission statement, this should feature in the annual report.

The one essential is always to look beyond your product to its application (i.e. communications – not publishing; transport – not railway operator; newsagent – simultaneously retailer and service provider). Perception is also important.

> What elements make up your corporate and brand identity, i.e. what do you stand for and how does this manifest itself?
> How does the company communicate its long- and short-term goals?
> What is the company's planned strategy to achieve these aims? How does the company plan to implement this strategy?

FINANCIAL DATA
The marketing director's areas of financial responsibility will vary from company to company. In a manufacturing environment, the director of manufacturing may have responsibility until the goods leave the factory gate, the sales director until they land on shelf, and the marketing director from then on, incentivizing the consumer to buy.

In reality, the lines are blurred. Whatever the case, the marketing director needs figures on production and manufacturing, plant, wages, research and development, administration and financing costs to build up a global picture before he attempts to pull together the costs which his department may incur.

MARKET BACKGROUND
It is not sufficient to know how you are performing in the marketplace. It is vital to know the performance of your competitors, in different geographic locations and towards different audiences. This is also the time to look at political and social pressures which have affected the market. Do you have proof that there is a market there to justify keeping your product or launching a new one? Are your products making enough money?

MARKETING AUDIT
Since the first three are relatively straightforward and should be readily available, let's look at the fourth, the audit. This should look at your product, your strengths and weaknesses, your organization. The idea is to acquire the information you need to make decisions without suffocating under computer print-outs. So what do you need?

First, satisfy yourself that your product fills a hole and could not be made to perform better through a redesign.

Second, ensure that its price relates to its quality.

Third, make sure that it is readily available at all the outlets which could sell it profitably.

Fourth, test the effectiveness of your promotional campaigns. It might be time to shift your money below as opposed to above the line, or to concentrate on more regional promotions.

Fifth, check how effective your sales team really is. How often do you review their training and motivation requirements?

MARKETING STRATEGY

Setting strategy calls for a clear head and the ability to transform information into long-term plans. It also means, in an international organization, ensuring that any goals which are transplanted from one country to another are workable.

A credit card may be a winner in the US, yet have far more problems in Europe due to the disparity of the markets and the competition. A trawl through the databases will track down relevant recent and historical background.

Then look at your marketing objectives and goals. Rank them, and be very clear how you are going to measure success and failure. As previously mentioned, the key phrase is accountability. If you database market, you can measure share, product usage, value, promotion and perceptions against a segment just for starters.

Check the systems you have in place to ensure that each marketing element is monitored regularly and problem solving becomes a speedy and automatic process. The process should also allow for investment in new product development and line extensions, so that opportunities are researched regularly.

Finally, check the strategy itself. If it hasn't worked, find out why and which elements need tinkering with. Some may function better in one region than in another.

IMPLEMENTATION PROGRAMME

The plan is in place, the schedule and the budgets set, yet there is no guarantee that the organization is ready to work to this plan. It needs to be talked through at all levels, to ensure that any change of culture is understood.

The process will need managing, and the lines of reporting need to be clearly defined. Are your team members up to the task, or do you need to acquire additional investment in training?

BUDGETS AND CONTINGENCIES

It is easy to allocate budgets, tougher to keep to them. Accurate forecasting must be carried out so that you don't run the risk of running over budget. In promotions, for example, particularly sponsorship, a sponsor looks at the up-front cost but rarely at the fact that the same sum will be needed again to support his investment in promotional terms.

Attempt to allocate a cost to each element, and add an additional sum for contingencies. Chances are you won't need it, but it helps, as will a contingency programme if your scheme doesn't run according to plan. The key is flexibility.

REALITY

Some companies, particularly small ones, find it hard to look at the broader picture. Corporate identity, strategy or an implementation plan may be just vague concepts. A marketing plan seems a luxury if you are too busy ensuring bills are paid. Yet the reality is that, without one, you'll never escape the treadmill.

A marketing department may consist of one person. This is not a handicap, particularly if that person has the ability to convey a sense of marketing culture throughout the company. It helps to understand who the customer is, what they want, and how you should provide that.

MARKETING PLAN CHECKLIST

The following can be used as a ready reckoner to ensure you have all the ammunition you need to plan.

Development data

Long-term objectives – brand or product extension

Short-term objectives – how do you intend to get there?

History – what are the problems that have beset such objectives in the past?

Future – what safeguards can you build in to prevent
   them in the future?
Competition
What profit is required to meet both short and long
   term objectives?
How do they fit into the corporate whole?
Budget – long- and short-term
Measurement
Methodology
Resources
Implementation
Programme revision

Research data
Market background
Sales figures
Salesforce figures
Demographics
Published information
Customer database

Measurement
How have you measured objectives in the past?
Sales
Brand switching
Awareness
Television Ratings (TVRs)
Column inches
Creation of new markets
Accountability – BS5750
Profitability

Can these be adjusted to set up standards for the future?

3

THE ROLE OF MARKET RESEARCH

The different types. Can it save money or is it worth going by gut feel?

Since the essence of marketing is customer knowledge, market research can be the most valuable tool in this quest. Information is not gathered solely by people on street corners, armed with clipboards and waiting to pounce at the most inappropriate moment. In fact, it was one of the industries most eager to invest in technology.

WHAT IS IT?

The Market Research Society provides a definition which seems to lack adequate punctuation. It is, it says, 'the collection, analysis, interpretation and presentation of information obtained from individuals or groups of people in order to guide decisions on a wide range of matters affecting consumers, either as buyers or as citizens.'

To put it more simply, market research is about people, what makes them tick now and what's likely to in the future. The discipline can then be broken down into two distinct types: quantitative and qualitative. Effective marketing is likely to need a combination of both.

Choosing the right course

There is always going to be a need for quantitative data. If you seek to convince a board or a bank manager of a project's potential merit, it's essential to provide the figures to back it. Yet those figures may just convey a snapshot of a market and potential consumers, they won't indicate what motivates them to buy your product. That is where qualitative research comes in.

One of the best examples to illustrate its strengths is one

of the earliest. It occurred in the US, where a food company was testing cake mixes. The company worried that it had shot itself in the foot. Housewives gave the thumbs down to a complete instant mix because, they felt, it would do them out of a job. However, research showed that if the firm removed the powdered egg and asked the consumer to add fresh ones, then they saw the mix as a labour-saving commodity.

Providing a pointer

Market research is not a universal panacea. It can provide pointers and suggest solutions, but how the information gathered is acted upon is always up to the client. Still, some questions you may want answered are:

1. Why are consumers buying a competitor's brand over our own?
2. What are they seeking in this market environment and are we providing it?
3. What will they look for next year, the year after, the year after that?
4. What is influencing changing tastes?
5. Who are our consumers, who are those of our competitors? Where do they live?
6. How will they react to new product development?

FIRST PORT OF CALL

Before commissioning any research, the first place to look is in-house. Sales figures are surprisingly under-used, particularly if they bear unpleasant news. Yet when analysed, often merged with other relevant bits of external data, they can provide pointers for why products fare less well in certain outlets, and to what extent timing is a factor.

This information can be used when formulating briefs, which should always be written. This is a safeguard in any marketing service work – progress can always be verified, cross checked, and signed off. It also ensures that any additional work will need client approval, and any extra budget agreed.

So, having worked out what information you have to hand, what else do you need? Probably the answers to some of the questions above, but this is where a skilled researcher can come in handy in formulating the brief. In fact, there are those who believe that market research should now be called marketing research. While the former describes the provision of data, the latter implies not just the collection of data but the ability to convert it into a vital piece of marketing ammunition.

The search for a market research supplier is not simple. There is no one company which is best for every project, so it is vital to do everything you can to ensure, as in *Hello Dolly*, that you make a perfect match.

CLIENT CHECKLIST
A supplier will need

> written brief
> concise problem in context
> preliminary meeting
> idea of what will be influenced by research results
> budget parameters
> timing considerations

You should ask supplier for

> proof of related expertise (and references)
> proof, through stating research objectives, that
>   they have understood the problem and their
>   role
> profiles of key personnel
> background on field operation
> data on maintaining quality control

information on methodology (covering any
preliminary work, data collection techniques,
what type and how many people will be
interviewed and how they will be selected)
projected cost and comprehensive breakdown
detailed timetable and reporting deadline
hardware and software data
information on reporting style (and guarantees of
just who will be working on the project)
information on project-management skill
data on billing procedures, accounting and legal
aspects
possibly proof of adherence to BS5750 standards

IS IT NECESSARY?

These are the basics, but they don't address whether or
not market research is truly necessary. There are argu-
ments on both sides. The German publisher Bauer, for
instance, has a well-known stable of women's magazines which it publishes throughout the Continent. It
has a successful formula and it sticks to it.

When it turned its attention to the UK, initially for the
launch of *Bella* magazine, the women's weekly market
was dominated by IPC. Yet Bauer saw a niche for itself,
for a lively yet low-cost publication. The amount of
market research it did prior to launch was marginal,
consisting mainly of focus groups. Instead it pumped
the majority of its budget into advertising – and it
worked.

HITS . . .

Consumers look to competitive pricing as an important
part of the decision-making process, yet are not prepared to sacrifice quality for pence. This is true in the
UK and abroad, so when Adams Childrenswear started
to look at the Continent for expansion it asked Research
International to study the market and its prospects. The

study highlighted the lack of any real quality mass-clothing retailers in Spain and the perception of Spanish-made goods as badly designed and outdated. It all pointed to a niche for a retailer offering quality, value and fashion. Adams' openings in Spain have proved the research right, allowing it to target its range more accurately and thus avoid costly failures.

... AND MISSES

The most dramatic failures for an industry are those which gain the biggest exposure. If a chocolate bar sinks without trace after launch, few, apart from those involved, will remember it two months down the line.

Yet when leading polling organizations fall four percentage points short of the General Election outcome, it's egg on face time. The use of more accurate sampling methods have been recommended in future, while secret ballots have been proposed as a way of overcoming people's reluctance to admit which way they intend to vote.

BARRIERS TO INNOVATION

Companies wishing to innovate through new product development face another problem. Many stress the need to run any new concept through a market research phase which includes a financial model. If it is a new product, creating a new market, how can it be tested against existing parameters? Those consultancies specializing in NPD view this is a major threat to innovation.

MINIMUM STANDARDS

So what does the client really want? Ideally, assurance of minimum standards to include data evaluation, interviewer recruitment and training. There is no point in having data if the results are tainted by mismanagement.

Clients may want to institute their own terms and conditions, particularly in a tender situation. In addition to some of the criteria supplied above, they may also be looking for evidence of creativity, relevance of data and added value.

SUPPLIER DIFFERENTIATION
Each supplier will have his own area of specialism, although the bigger firms will have far more strings to their bows than their smaller brethren. Some will promote their adherence to BS5750, involving set procedures, working practices and quality standards. The trouble is that clients don't know how much store to set by this standard.

As a general rule of thumb:

- don't ask whether a firm works to BS5750 unless you understand what it involves in practical terms
- even if your company demands BS5750, make it your duty to understand its effect on suppliers in practical terms
- it is unwise to discriminate against those firms which don't possess BS5750, yet have proven qualities of project management, references, good quality procedures, and offer added value.

DISCRIMINATING DATA
Earlier in this chapter I mentioned sales data, one of the biggest assets the client owns. The danger is, however, of regarding it as one-dimensional data. A researcher can transform the data into a multi-faceted aid.

Take lifestyle profiling. It adds flesh to the definition of customers, identifying them as individuals rather than households or geographical groups which is where inaccurate assumptions can be made through generalizations.

You might want to use profiling to confirm just who your customers are, to ensure you are targeting the right people using the right methods. Alternatively you might want to identify specific niche markets previously unexploited.

TECHNOLOGY BOOSTER

As mentioned at the beginning of this chapter, the market research industry has been an enthusiastic advocate of new technology. Those commissioning market research for the first time might like to understand some of the jargon, and the benefits.

First, take Computer Aided Telephone Interviewing (CATI). This is particularly useful for international campaigns, when it can prove cheaper to ring from a central source. CATI offers the ability to build in as many quality checks as necessary, depending on whether the client wants data that is as accurate as possible or a less costly pointer.

Computerized Personal Interviewing (CAPI), where survey questionnaires are pre-programmed on to a floppy or a hard disk, for use by interviewers with laptops, has revolutionized the industry. All interviewers need to do is keep an eye on the script and key in answers. When the survey is complete, the data is transmitted electronically to the receiving computer.

Computerization has a number of benefits. Consistent quality and accuracy are assured because the results are downloaded instead of transcribed manually, and the computer can backcheck to weed out respondents giving false answers, warning the interviewer to bring the interview to an early close.

MYSTERY SHOPPING

One aspect of research has grown substantially in recent years: it is in the area of mystery shopping. In retail, executives often visit their outlets unannounced to find out what greets their customers. The research industry has merely formalized this practice, briefing trained evaluators before they visit an outlet, and recording their experiences in as precise and objective a way as possible.

Mystery shoppers can record

> how long it takes them to get served
> how staff greet them
> how staff gauge what product/service to offer
> the suitability of products offered
> the courtesy, or lack of it, displayed by staff
> how the transaction was concluded

The benefit of mystery shopping is that it records the facts from an encounter, rather than what people think or remember, the outcome of conventional research. Such research is not done in an underhand way since outlets are usually forewarned, although with no details of time and place. Even so, researchers are hard to spot since they will have been picked to match the consumer profile exactly.

4

RESEARCH AND SETTING OBJECTIVES

It's all very well aiming at the moon, but is it worth it, can you achieve it, and how will you know when you get there?

In any area of marketing, quite apart from planning, the actual setting of objectives can be the most crucial part of the operation. Nobody said it was going to be easy, particularly in an integrated campaign where each element needs a different form of measurement, yet neither is it impossible as many would have you believe.

A CHALLENGE

The setting of objectives should be regarded as a challenge. If you want your brand to achieve brand leadership, you need to answer questions like when and for how long. Only then do you look at how you can achieve it, and what means you will use.

If you are dealing with a can of beer, and the timing is next month for a month, the strategy could well be promotion, focusing on a sudden burst of advertising and a price-cut offer. If we hit a hot spell, your production capacity is up to the challenge and the product isn't too obnoxious, then sales may well surge. What they won't do is stay there.

Success and failure mean different things to different people. In the mid-1970s, until the arrival of Cedric Scroggs from Cadbury to head up Leyland Cars new central marketing organization, success was rated by share, i.e. how cars fared against competitive models. This meant that a Jaguar, say, had to compete on price with a Mercedes. Yet since there were no figures on how much it cost to build a Jaguar, it was impossible to compute how much profit was made by any car. Scroggs first task was to create a team of four marketing managers, each one responsible for the annual profits of the models they controlled.

This example illustrates what happens when a company is under pressure to produce results. Seeing volume and market penetration as the objectives, without profit being built adequately into the equation, can play havoc with a company's reputation and financial stability.

HOW TO MEASURE

The challenge all clients face is measuring performance. Those who know the identity of their customers have a considerable advantage over those who have to go through a third party: they can track sales from start to finish. If there is an intermediary, a retailer, the process is not nearly so clear cut.

This is best explained by way of an example. Take a company selling a compilation album direct, bypassing the shops. It wants to appeal to men and women, it's country and western, and the age band is fairly broad. (It could just as easily be a bank, with a new deposit account geared to young savers. These could be university age or younger.) It has the budget to advertise in the press and on TV, but the brand owner wants proof of what is working, and where, so that he can adjust future campaigns accordingly. Yet how to isolate the components?

What needs to be done is to measure where the advertising process increases sales. The one aspect to bear in mind is that with hard data – you can do anything. All you need are honest figures, if there are such things. Maybe the best way is to look at it as a recipe.

1. Sales data

Crack a few heads to break down sales data by day, week, month (i.e. however long it is before the campaign starts), and continue for the duration of the campaign. Also isolate an area as a control, if possible, one where you perform no promotional activity.

Remember that sales data is what you are measuring performance against. What you are going by is the change in sales – the question is whether you see that change as part of the process or as something affected by the process.

Is increased sales your sole objective, or is the campaign part of a process called sales? It depends whether your sales force are just order takers or good sales people. If awareness changes form part of your objective, they cannot be measured using the recipe format, which deals only with tangibles.

2. Media spend
Work out the spend by the brand first by media title, then by TV region, and finally by region for other above-the-line media such as posters, cinema and radio, if applicable. With posters you might split it by looking at how many posters are available per region.

3. NRS (National Readership Survey) Media
Add a good dose of NRS Media data, which measure press readership, commercial TV viewing figures, cinema and the bigger radio stations by demographics like ACORN or geodemographics. It will profile the audiences.

This is as good an opportunity as any to debunk demographics. The confusion over measuring data, or even setting parameters, often lies in lack of understanding not just of demographics but of geodemographics, too. Demographics relates to people, who they are and where they live. Geodemographics is about understanding the characteristics of neighbourhoods, the type of people living within them and where.

You can't have demographics of business – it is an anomaly but it is wrong. It is possible to collate data about business, classifications and descriptions, but not demographics.

4. Mailing coverage
Stir in a copy of the mailing files, by full postcode, to look at the demographics of that geography. This covers you for the direct marketing side of the campaign. It is the binding agent to the recipe.

5. Door to door schedules
Add in the separate components of a door to door campaign, i.e. the schedule for targeting postcode sectors, the ACORN profile of the household in the targeted distribution, plus the spend on distribution.

6. Geography/Coverage
Distributors are usually regionalized though there is always a skew depending on which one you use. This is where you can create your control. If it is only available in certain areas, those are where it will be.

COOKING METHOD
It is possible, when combining all of the above data and using the services of a competent database marketing company, to work out whether you are achieving your objectives on a number of different levels. We can break this down into a two-stage operation.

First, it is possible to build a media spend profile by ACORN, or any of the other demographic classifications, for the UK. In time, this data can also be analysed in more detail, as more figures become available, say by region.

This can produce, by whatever demographic classification you choose, the number of households according to your own regional classifications, and the number of customers within each segment at the beginning of the period of measurement and then the number of new customers (since the media spend).

It could appear on a data sheet as follows:

Household type	xx
Total household	xxxx
Original customers	xxxxxxx
New customers	xx
Average spend (£)	
Old cus.	xxx
New cus.	xxx

The second stage will provide the same data but graded according to TV region, to determine the effectiveness of the media campaign. This might use either BARB (Broadcasters' Audience Research Board) or NRS figures, taking into account the regional spend by media and regional NRS reports.

DEALING WITH INTANGIBLES

So much for objectives which deal with sales rises (or falls) and where the customer is known. But what of the rest? Are there any pointers for how to deal with, say, measuring PR? The answer is that each day brings yet another method, some new natty software programmes, but the problem is subjectivity. What one person considers a good PR campaign, another could slam.

The best tip, apart from vetting each scheme that comes your way extremely carefully, while asking for and following up client referrals, is to set up a nine-point plan.

1. When writing the brief, itemize the objective(s) for each activity and the communication methods involved
2. Turn all objectives into targets which can be measured rather than relying on anecdotal information

3. Work out how you will rate media exposure and non-media activity and fix targets to be reached
4. Bear in mind that effective PR doesn't just mean media coverage
5. In a campaign using more than one medium or communication method, rate success by asking those who reply where they saw reference, to determine what it was advertising or editorial
6. Monitor the performance of rivals
7. When using a PR consultancy, or an in-house team, monitor campaign performance by holding regular meetings or keeping in touch by phone
8. Ask for contact and status reports
9. Keep agency on its toes by conducting agency appraisal meetings every quarter

COST

There is one major barrier to determining the effectiveness of a campaign: it's likely to cost money. Since advertising has always cost more, agencies have more experience in commissioning research to justify expenditure. Public relations, however, has never been such a bulk buyer.

Now that accountability has become so vital, all this may change. After all, it only needs the research industry to bring costs to an acceptable level for clients to agree to effectiveness monitoring being built into project budgets at the planning stage.

IS PR MEASURABLE?

Two aspects are worth considering. One is the number of mentions in the media, or opportunities to see (OTS). These may be misleading, since they have to be weighed against column length, inclusion and size of accompanying picture, and the publication itself, let alone whether the mention was flattering or not.

Another is an attempt to rate the media coverage in

terms of what it could have cost if it came from the advertising budget, in effect, the equivalent ad spent. Funnily enough, if you get a PR consultancy to assess this, it always works out at more than you would have been able to afford.

5

STRATEGY

Co-ordinating information and departments into a successful formula – who are you marketing to? The role of consultancies.

The trouble with strategy is that the world doesn't stand still. In a stable economy, strategic planning thrives as companies turn to market analysis to pinpoint new opportunities. When the going gets tough, the tendency is for a company to pull in its horns, rely on what has worked before, and return to financial analysis as its bedrock.

It is a dangerous route, but tempting if a company lacks a chief with the vision to see beyond his backyard. It also calls into question what strategy actually is. Here's one definition from the Oxford English Dictionary.

'*Strategy*. The art of a commander-in-chief; the art of projecting and directing the larger military movements and operations of a campaign. Usually distinguished from *tactics*, which is the art of handling forces in battle or in the immediate presence of the enemy.'

Unfortunately, there is a dearth of those who possess such vision and even fewer who can carry along the rest of the company on a tide of enthusiasm. The difficulties of this task were illustrated by Dr Lars Ramqvist, president and chief executive officer of Ericsson, at the 1994 UK Innovation Lecture.

'I had to meet with a number of investors on Wall Street to tell them about our continued, expanded R&D programmes. Obviously my message was clear – less short-term profit, but hopefully a brighter future for Ericsson. In other words perseverance and maybe some courage. Because what I told them was that Ericsson would be spending almost fifteen times as much on development as on dividends to the shareholders.'

THREE-STAGE PLAN
The OED definition is somewhat outdated. If we were to take the military analogy further, it implies there are three stages in preparing for war. The first is the ultimate aim. What do you wish to achieve? The second is the game plan. The third is the development of tactics for use on the battlefield. Unfortunately, the textbooks don't tell you that if you lumber through these phases any marketing opportunity will probably have passed you by when finally you come up with a strategy.

STRATEGY ON A PEDESTAL
The danger of setting a strategy is to set it in stone, to prepare it with inadequate input from those on the ground, and to take an age over it. Some companies navel gaze for years, only to find themselves overtaken by speedier competitors. The winners are likely to be those prepared to take risks, make mistakes, and empathize with their markets.

THE ALTERNATIVES
So far we have been talking about the 'top down' approach. It's not the only one, however, and since there are few visionaries the 'bottom up' approach has gained in popularity. Here, soundings are taken by the top from different divisions and formulated into plans which capitalize on a company's strengths. The eventual master strategy is likely to be more marketing oriented, since there has been input from those with more direct contact with customers, and more timely.

Alternatives in chart form
If we were to try and split the different stages into a chart form, they might look like this.

Top down
1. I have a dream
2. Who will make it work?
3. What effect will it have?
4. What relevant data is there?
5. Programme build up
6. Test, and rejig accordingly
7. Implementation, reassess

Bottom up
1. What are we good at?
2. What does customer/trade want?
3. Marry two into gameplan
4. Sort out tactics, market research
5. Test, and rejig accordingly
6. Implement
7. Assess against objectives/rejig

THE FUTURE
The only problem with the above two is that they imply fixed strategy, dangerous in a world moving as fast as ours. In the opening chapters, we talked of the need to database market, allowing strategy to be influenced by data flowing in on a continuous basis. Yet the organizational structure has to exist to allow this to happen.

It takes courage, because it means that strategic priorities will always be under review. A good example is industrial conglomerate Unilever. It is increasing investment in those categories which promise rapid growth, such as skin care, ice creams and top fragrances, and in those markets in Asia, Eastern Europe and South America which are expanding rapidly.

Under the chairmanship of Sir Michael Perry, it has also shaken up the way it handles marketing on a national basis. In the interests of greater efficiency, flexibility and speed of response it has formed regional and global marketing structures, regional innovation centres, and devoted a greater spend to IT. The overwhelming impression is of a company which knows it cannot afford to stand still.

Even its strategy for dealing with the threat from own brands breaks new ground. In Perry's Advertising Association President's Lecture, he announced his belief that the future lies with 'a new partnership with retailers'. He sees Unilever brands as an asset for retailers, which if they choose they can use as a model to improve their own margins.

CUSTOMER DEFINITION

A major problem when setting strategy is confusion over the definition of 'customer'. It is rare, if not impossible, for a company only to deal with one set of customers. Manufacturers, for example, often encounter as big a problem selling in to retailers as selling on to customers.

It is up to the marketing professional to explore and nurture the relationship with customers. Even though all staff should do more than pay lip service to fulfilling customer needs, it is the marketer who is responsible for understanding and interpreting them.

'We must therefore market marketing, certainly as a culture and more effectively as strategy, since it is surely no longer possible to differentiate corporate strategy from market strategy. At the tactical level, leading edge know-how must be transferred to those who wish to enter the profession.'

Professor Michael J. Thomas, Senior Vice-Chairman CIM, Professor of Marketing at the University of Strathclyde.

ROLE OF STRATEGY

As described in Chapter 4, there is more than one way to judge success. The role of strategy, however, has to be involved with growing profit even if this means a corporate culture change. Focus on six key areas when looking at future strategy.

Markets Like Unilever, select those countries experiencing growth, and those product sectors which are still expanding. Research the demographics, customer attitudes and lifestyles

Market share Never forget that it is people who will provide you with increased sales, so look beyond product and price

Staff Invest in the people who will personify your corporate culture, both in terms of salary, training, motivation and conditions of employment

Innovate Create new markets which you can own, at least for a time, before the competition catches up, and try to grow existing markets

Technology Maintain investment in this area as a step towards cutting costs and improving communication throughout the firm

Add value Research shows that customers look for improved quality as well as value for money. Beware of focusing too much on cost reduction since consumers could be just as interested in added value, and will be prepared to pay for it.

ROLE OF CONSULTANTS

So far we have talked about companies formulating strategy, but this neglects one important fact: when to look outside for assistance. This is particularly applicable if there is a takeover, merger, or a senior board appointment in a traditionally run company.

In these instances, the temptation is to seek the services

of an external consultant. This has a number of advantages. One of the major ones is that someone coming in to the situation cold can often see the wood for the trees. Yet it also has advantages in terms of pushing decisions through. A consultant may get a better hearing at board level precisely because they are being paid large sums of money than someone on the payroll, even though the advice they are giving may be the same.

There is another plus. If the advice is contentious, or if it might provoke a personality clash when delivered by an internal staff member, the use of a consultant can avoid unpleasantness and stand a greater chance of success. Clients can also take advantage of the fact that consultants cover a great many businesses and sectors, and will use their extensive and up to date knowledge to provide a broader overview than might otherwise have been possible.

Consultant downside
Consultants often find themselves on a hiding to nothing if senior management has not been able to persuade middle management or the rest of the staff of the benefits of hiring outside help. They encounter antagonism because of their perceived cost and may have problems in gathering information internally.

The flip side of being able to see the wood for the trees is that consultants will never become immersed totally in company culture. They also have the added disadvantage that they won't be on the spot if it proves to be a long-term programme, while their contract was short-term. Internal staff might have more success in gaining access to the board, in which case they will have to sell the consultant's advice on, always a dangerous course.

THINK GLOBAL, ACT LOCAL
A much misused phrase, but just how do you organize if you wish to start selling overseas? You will need people

on the ground to market and distribute your product, but can you afford to set up your own operation, the best option, or will you have to rely on an independent distributor? It may be that you know of a company tapping the same markets, and you can piggyback on to its operations. No matter which route you choose, there are going to be a number of strategic points to bear in mind:

Community feeling
As the Japanese car makers have done in this country, it may be necessary to introduce local manufacturing to overcome political and consumer resistance

Flexibility
A package which works in one country may need tailoring to suit another, either adding or substituting elements

Security
A customer buying a foreign product will wish to be re-assured of a local outlet providing after sales service

Turn chameleon
It could be in your best interests to play down the fact that you own a local company in markets which are fiercely nationalistic, often those in the former Eastern Bloc.

THE HUB
So what should the strategic role of the centre be? It will, of course, vary from firm to firm but there should be some constants. The centre should try to maintain quality by putting staff they can trust into local environments and monitoring performance. They should keep them motivated, and use the knowledge they cull from different markets to improve performance and build strategy. Above all, the centre should keep an open mind as to the strategy which will work abroad. A flexible regime is always more effective than a rigid one.

ADVERTISING

The most obvious, and expensive, way of influencing your market

So far we've talked about the company, the product, the market. Now for the first time we move on to opening up a dialogue with the customer. It may be a bit one-sided – a two-way conversation is really the province of direct marketing – but it's a start.

Historically, there have always been two types of advertising, namely above and below-the-line, with a myriad of sub-categories. The terms relate to accounting practices. Ad agencies used to direct all promotional activity, advertising was seen as their main function so it appeared above the line on expenditure reports, while everything else was lumped together as promotions and appeared below.

FOCUS ON CUSTOMER
By now you know the customers' likes and dislikes – your ads must respond to their needs. Sometimes those ads must focus on needs which they didn't even know they had. Yet it is worthwhile bearing one fact in mind, as follows.

PRODUCT PLUS
Promotion is one of the four essential elements in marketing – the four 'P's. Yet it is not worth spending money on if the product itself is unmarketable. Advertising may prompt a consumer to trial once or twice, but repeat buys are out if the product is not attuned to its market.

Investing in intangibles
Advertising works better in some areas then others, but it can be just as effective promoting a service or a charity

as a product. In effect, it can add flesh to a service that consumers can identify with. Charities rarely have the budget for massive media campaigns, but the Lottery may change that.

Multi-faceted campaigns
Ads can work on different levels to different audiences, but the key is **consistency**.

Look at some of the corporate campaigns around. At one level they can inspire confidence in the City, at another reassure internal staff, suppliers, maybe even retailers, and at yet another build the loyalty of their customers. The only constraint is that the messages must not conflict with one another, nor with those of any brands owned by the corporation.

INTEGRATED MARKETING
It is dangerous to look at advertising in isolation. It is only one part of the marketing mix, and requires a fair degree of management skill to ensure that the sales promotion message backs up that of the advertising, the direct marketing, the public relations, etc. Not least, the product has to be available in sufficient quantities when the demand is stimulated.

COST COMPARISONS
The choice of sales methods will vary according to budget, distribution, product, and audience. The choice, however, isn't that extensive:

Sales force
More on this section later, but suffice to say it is expensive, as any labour intensive method is, and rapidly giving way or made more efficient by database marketing

Above the line
An expensive choice, and can you be absolutely sure of hitting your market with a scattergun approach?

Below the line
Less costly, depending on choice of disciplines, and also
on the quality of the lists you are using for direct mail or
telemarketing. A duff list may be more costly than
going above the line.

MASS MARKET MAYHEM
Mass market brands have, in the past, used mass market
media. The winds of change are blowing, however.
Heinz, for example, has come to recognize the power of
direct/database marketing and though this currently
leaves its TV budget unaffected it will have an impact
on just how it uses the medium. It is likely to opt for
commercials whose impact is easier to measure.

The other factor behind such moves is the question
mark which hangs over mass media. Do they really
provide the mass audiences of old, since with the coming of cable and satellite the market has grown so frag-
mented? Television and press are too powerful to aban-
don, but clients are increasingly adding response
mechanisms to campaigns in these media to ensure they
get more bangs for their bucks.

THE ROLE OF ADVERTISING
What can it do for you? Hopefully, raise awareness,
promote brand switching, build loyalty and of course
increase sales. That's the good news. What it won't do
is achieve all these simultaneously. You must:

Set realizable objectives
Ensure they don't conflict
Measure results
Not rely on agency to provide all campaign data
– and to measure its own effectiveness

International advertising
The growth of global brands and marketing has
prompted a rise in the number of international campaigns seen on screen. Whether it has prompted a

higher level of creativity or effectiveness is a moot point. It only needs a glance at the winners of recent international advertising competitions to realize they rely heavily on humour, sometimes slapstick, and are in danger of appealing to the lowest common denominator.

If this is the future face of advertising, it would be wise to look at some of the pitfalls:

> think global, act local does not mean dubbing a commercial so it works in different languages
> it needs strong imagery to work, and possibly fewer words. Look at Benetton. You may not like it, but it raises awareness
> ensure your agency can control quality in each country, or that you or your local agents have the wherewithal to do so. You won't necessarily get a second chance
> a campaign may work the whole world over but it's rare. Allow for local customs. The Oil of Ulay 'Apple' campaign gained an internal award from Saatchi, yet had to be adapted for the Middle East.

STAY IN TOUCH

Some agencies fail to stay in touch with reality – it's worthwhile avoiding them. The head of one knew it was time to move on when his team presented a high profile, mega bucks campaign, guaranteed – they claimed – to build the client an image second to none. Trouble was, the client did not have an infinite budget and just wanted to shift products on the high street.

Checklist

Any client would be advised to keep that old journalist's mainstay in mind: the who, what, when, where, how and why.

Who is the audience?
What is the product – and its unique selling point?
When does a campaign need to be launched, and what other factors, such as production, distribution, or other promotions need to be built into the equation?
Where does the campaign need to run to achieve maximum effect, and within budget?
How will the objectives be measured and maintained?
Why are you running the campaign in the first place?

MEDIA RANGE
What is the choice, when looking at media? The mainstay comprises

> television (terrestrial, cable, satellite) and within this section is also a choice of soft or hard sell, sponsored TV versus Direct Response TV (DRTV)
> press (national and regional papers, consumer and trade magazines, advertorials/promotions, etc.)
> outdoor (posters)
> radio
> cinema

In each of these you will be looking at their reach and frequency, possibly relying on advice from your agency, audience research, and whether it fits the brief.

The constraining factors will be:

> budget
> audience profile
> message itself
> timing

THE AGENCY
Choosing an advertising agency can be a time-consuming, frustrating and stimulating task. As the industr has grown, so the structure of agencies has

altered to adapt. In the past, you would expect to deal with your account team, who would be served by the creative department, whose achievements would gain exposure by virtue of the media buying department.

Rigid delineation, however, led to inefficiencies and re-duced competitiveness. An account team will now in-clude creatives, while media buying is more important than ever before – often the function of an independent agency. A roster of big advertising clients results in more competitive prices being charged for space and airtime.

Indeed, the two most important people working on a client's business are the account planner, who brings an understanding of the consumer, the decision-making process, etc., and the media planner. The latter has an in-depth knowledge of how the defined target audience consumes media and how best these consumers can be reached. The one team member whose role has decreased is the account manager. It may be a bit harsh to call him a 'glorified administrator' but, on occasions, this is how his role has evolved.

Media research and planning, in the mid-1980s in danger of becoming a fringe activity, has become an in-tegral part of the process.

What to look for?
You may want increased sales, you may want enhanced awareness, but what is it going to take for an agency to come up with the goods? The following are some of the qualities you should look for in the agency, the order in which you put them depends on your brief. The danger is in assigning too low a priority to creativity and too high to value for money.

Calibre of account and media planners
Creativity
Financial results
Intellect and flexibility
International expertise
Marketing strategy
Media buying
Media planning
Value for money

THE FUTURE

As stated at the beginning of this chapter, the question advertisers and agencies are having to face up to is what effect will not just cable and satellite have on advertising, but also pay-per-view, video-on-demand, subscription TV and interactive media? Few agencies are up to speed with technology changes and how to write advertising for it.

Edwin Artzt, chairman and chief executive of Procter and Gamble, spoke at the American Association of Advertising Agencies conference in 1994 of his fear that new media could bar access to whole market segments.

They may, but there again audiences in the UK see advertising as an art form. There is no reason why commercials should not appear on pay-per-view and interactive media. The question is what sort of audiences will they provide, how much will it cost to reach them, and what forms of commercials will be effective, particularly in interactive media?

The US cable home shopping channel, QVC, has shown that the amount viewers/shoppers spend with it has more relevance than ratings. In the future the needs of these shoppers will change, and they will want immediate access to shots of the items they are interested in rather than waiting for them as they do at present. The challenge is to meet these needs instead of rushing in to transfer one media to another and call it 'inter-active' or 'multimedia'.

Clients should not be afraid of new media, they should just be clear as to their needs and those of their customers. Some of the best of these media are niche markets and tightly targeted, offering segmentation opportunities, reduced wastage and cost efficiency unavailable elsewhere.

7

SALES PROMOTION

A way to make money, add value, or both? The role of pricing

Sales promotion has, for a long time, been dogged with the title of poor relation in the marketing world. In reality, though, the days of the tacky giveaway disappeared as customers expressed a desire for true added value.

Its rate of growth outstrips that of above-the-line advertising as clients turn to it to fulfil not just tactical but strategic objectives. It has the added advantage of being easily measurable.

WHAT IS IT?

According to the industry's body, the Institute of Sales Promotion (ISP):

'Sales promotion comprises a range of tactical marketing techniques designed within a strategic marketing framework to add value to a product or service in order to achieve specific sales and marketing objectives.'

So much for the strict definition, but it doesn't help the general public, who still don't have a great understanding of sales promotion. They see it as a free cassette, a competition for a place at a major sporting event. In fact, the range of activities which consultants in this area now cover is fairly extensive. It includes conference and exhibition work; sales force/incentives and product placement. True, some of these are dealt with by PR consultants, too, but the objective of the client is not always pure media coverage.

Drawing the line

The problem with sales promotion, direct marketing and public relations is just where to draw the line. If an on-pack offer uses the names and addresses of those who write in in future mailings, is it sales promotion or direct marketing?

Mechanics
The list of sales promotion techniques is endless, but these are some of the main manifestations:

> On-pack offers
> Coupons
> Sampling
> Price cuts
> Premium offers (more produce per pack/two for the price of one)
> Competitions
> Vouchers
> Free gifts/free mail-ins
> Clubs
> Points systems
> Card loyalty schemes
> Magazines
> Point of sale
> Cross-brand promotions
> Self-liquidating offer
> Loss leader
> Trade force incentives
> Door to door
> Banded offers

Some of these are variations on others. A points system may lead to a free gift, for example, while a club can lead to sampling opportunities and money-off vouchers. A retailer magazine can offer consumers added value, money off vouchers, information and competitions.

Effectiveness
It will depend on a number of factors:

creativity
timing
efficient targeting
budget

There is no guarantee. The most worrying aspect is re-demptions – where over- or under-redeeming can be financially punitive. Insuring against either can be as costly as the event itself, so it is advisable to take advice from a consultancy with a good track record.

Sales Promotion Industry

The industry has prospered because it understands what motivates different audiences. Direct marketing, mean-while, knows how to reach those audiences so the growing rapprochement between the two is a logical step.

Maybe distinctions between the two disciplines matter not a jot. After all, if you go to a sales promotion con-sultancy with an aim which could only be fulfilled by a direct marketing mechanic, would the consultant turn the business down even though he may not possess a direct marketing qualification? He's more likely to seek professional advice in this area. And if the promotion performs the task who cares what heading it comes under, anyway?

As in any marketing activity, clients should look at the background, the objectives, the budget, the planning and the evaluation of a project's success.

Let's take it step by step.

1. What is the objective?

increased sales?
loyalty?
brand switching?

      trialling?
      loyalty?
      awareness?
      information?

2. Is it compatible with the role of sales promotion?

3. If the answer is yes, move on to the budgeting stage.

4. Budgeting:

i)   How much money is in the kitty?
ii)   This will, at the very least, have to cover communication, fulfilment and contingency costs as well as agency fees. What about legal advice, additional artwork, etc?
iii) How much is going to be available for each one?
iv) When moving into planning stage, split budget by element and phase. Look, for instance, at set-up and fulfilment costs.
v)   What redemption rate are you budgeting for?
vi) Project management is key. Shop around for value for money, and when you have achieved it any alterations to schedule and costings should be signed by client and agency.
vii) At the end of the campaign, did you run over or within budget? What lessons can be learned?

5. Planning:

i)   Produce rounded brief
ii)   Look at brand in context of market. What hampers growth? What could help it?
iii) Return to objective(s). Add precise targets you wish to reach.
iv) What techniques can you afford?

v) What communication channels are appropriate/ within budget?
vi) How do these facts mesh with what will appeal to customer?

6. Evaluation:

i) This will depend on original objectives. Sales is the most obvious, comparing it with a control, in areas where the promotion did not run, and also looking at other data in comparable periods. The most obvious sources are AGB and Nielsen.
ii) Redemption levels are key, but should be seen in the broader context of additional sales. If they do not hit target, how will you know, before the end of the promotion, the reason why? Researching throughout is vital, and may enable you to rescue a potential failure.

Evaluation problems

Some problems are still common to the sales promotion industry. Clients ask the discipline to achieve too many different objectives and fail to isolate exactly what data is useful for evaluation purposes. The result is a woolly brief and evaluation is cut short when the budget runs out.

Point of reference

The industry body, the ISP, has already been quoted in this chapter, but there is another association which is just as useful to potential sales promotion users. This is the Sales Promotion Consultants Association (SPCA), which represents the leading UK sales promotion consultants.

It has three main aims:

To demonstrate to promoters the benefits of

        employing the services of SPCA member
        consultancies

To ensure that clients enjoy the highest
professional and ethical standards of
consultancy service and execution from
member consultancies

To support and assist member companies in the
achievement of these standards.

Role of Sales Promotion

As discussed earlier, sales promotion is more than just a tactical tool. The danger lies in choosing it for its potential rather than for a project or a strategic need. The table at the end of the chapter provides a handy reckoner on what mechanics can be used for which problems, but it is just a guide.

To recap, then, what is the role of sales promotion? Some would argue it is to make money, others that it is to ensure budgets are spent most effectively. Both, in the long term, would be right. If you're ready to roll, just check the following before proceeding.

1. Are your objective(s) clearly defined?
2. Have you determined the current position of brand or service against major rivals?
3. Are you sure that there is a role for sales promotion or might another discipline be more appropriate?
4. Have you proof that you have highlighted appropriate technique/communications channel to achieve aim?
5. Will you remember to refine objective(s) in light of analysis?
6. Have you weighed up the cost of techniques/communication channels against budget and potential effectiveness and have you built in a contingency budget?

Legal, decent, honest and truthful

There are legal requirements for each area of promotional marketing, and the list of associations at the end of the book will provide a contact point for those wishing to know more.

In sales promotion, while the majority of schemes are legal, there will always be those which fall through the net. Consumers will be familiar with the promotion which insists that no purchase is required, yet often it is. The way round it is to offer those who write in tokens or entry forms for the price of a self-addressed envelope. The other area disputed is when a contest of skill turns into a game of chance. Promoters using premium telephone lines have been taken to task more than once.

Sales promotion aims	Boost buying rate	Boost consumer loyalty	Boost distribution	Boost penetration	Boost repeat sales	Buy bigger	Grow traffic	Heighten awareness (consumer)	Promote display	Shift large stocks
Banded packs	X			X						X
Buy one, get one free/twin packs		X								
Competitions	X				X					
Coupons (discount choice)		X								
Free draws								X		
Free gifts/trial							X			
Free offers	X			X	X					X
Price slash									X	
In-store raffle/competition	X									X
In-store merchandizing				X						X
Money-off coupons/offers		X		X			X			
Crossbrand promotions	X		X	X		X				
On-pack money off coupons			X							

On-pack premiums

Personality promotions

Phone-ins

Premium offers

Reduced price offers

Refund offers

Refund/buyback offers

Reusable container premiums

Salesforce incentives

Sample distribution

Sampling

Self-liquidating premiums

Shareouts/giveaways

Sweepstakes

Tailormade promotions

Trade competitions

8

DIRECT AND DATABASE MARKETING

The quickest and most accurate route to your customer – if handled properly. Don't forget telemarketing. How not to waste a fortune.

Direct marketing is not a topic that often hits the headlines unless mentioned in connection with two words that haunt the industry – 'junk mail'. It is, however, an industry that has seen unprecedented growth.

What is the reason for this expansion? It's not an area which attracts fans because of its creativity and ease of use (although the former is alive and well, just not much in evidence). More pertinent, however, is the fact that direct marketing is effective, and with advances in new technology growing more so daily.

The main reason for growth is likely to be a combination of three factors: media fragmentation, computers that are growing more powerful and cheaper year on year, and the need to find and retain loyal customers. After all, 90 per cent of profit is said to come from repeat purchasers and the rest from triallists. It is more cost-effective to keep those you've got.

The main elements of direct marketing are:

> direct mail
> direct response advertising: TV, press or radio
>   (freephone number)
> inserts (with a coupon)
> telemarketing
> door-to-door distribution
> interactive media

WHAT IS IT?
As in all the disciplines, definitions abound. In fact, the leading American tome, Direct Marketing Magazine,

used to carry one and a half pages on the subject in each issue commissioned from three industry experts.

The simplest comes from the doyen of the industry, Drayton Bird, who claims that direct marketing is:

'Any advertising activity which creates and exploits a direct relationship between you and your prospect or customer as an individual'

There is a simile, however, which gives it a much more human face. Think of direct marketing as a corner shop, which gives you the kind of service that has gone out of fashion. The owners know everything about you, your likes and dislikes, family birthdays, what your family buys, whether you pay cash or on credit.

HOW DOES IT WORK?

Direct marketing requires one essential ingredient: accurate data about those you are marketing too, historical and current, about the market you are operating in, and about the product or service itself. All too often the glue that binds it together with an effective means of communicating with this audience is the **database**.

The danger, as discussed earlier, lies in pigeonholing databases with lists and direct marketing when their role is much greater. Companies have a tendency to dip a toe in the water and see them as providing a personalized list. But to embrace the concept is to introduce database marketing and build your business around it. In the 1990s, it will prove the only way to grow it.

WHY DIRECT MARKETING?

Why should you use direct marketing? These are the most persuasive reasons:

Cost-effective communication, if used properly

Customer service

Price

Delivery of a 'pure' message, unaffected by
media or rivals

Streamlined delivery

It is measurable, gauging impact, response, sales
and incremental margin, giving it a head start
against other media channels

Two-way, an invaluable dialogue

Loyalty builder

ROLE OF MEASUREMENT

Another of direct marketing's assets is the ability to pre-test campaigns and other marketing initiatives. All the best companies test, hardly surprising when the results are so dramatic. When test marketing a new product through direct marketing, one company registered that the best marketing proposition was 58 times more effective than the worst. So what does measuring success tell us?

'In the absence of significant experience of product and market, testing is vital to determine strategy. Without testing you are guessing. Without testing you are producing fewer sales and lower profits. Without testing you are not learning. You are not learning what works and what does not. You are not learning what motivates the customer, what beats the competition.'

Stewart Pearson, Chief Executive, PPHN at ISBA conference,
June 1994

There is a role for both qualitative and quantitative research in this area. While the latter tells you who responds, and perhaps more importantly, who does not respond, qualitative research can help in formulating the right message for the right customer.

MEDIA
Direct mail

This is the best known of the media, with direct response advertising running a close second. It is suitable for consumer and business-to-business marketing and, despite the hype, is often a preferred communication channel compared with, say, individual salesman pressure or an ad with space to tell only half the story.

But don't let anybody tell you it is cheap. It comes second only to telemarketing in this respect. A TV or Press campaign can deliver greater numbers more cheaply than either, but the flip side is that they won't necessarily be the right people.

Pros
Accurate targeting
Control over message and timing
Flexible format

Cons
Can be one-dimensional
Lack of creativity
Difficulty of finding the right list

Direct mail campaign checklist
1. Set objectives
2. Set budget
3. Plan campaign elements
4. Segment audience
5. Find names
6. Brief creatives
7. Concept stage
8. Draw up production schedule
9. Brief suppliers (internal and external)
10. Evaluate results

Direct response advertising
The best aspect of print and broadcast media is the data on readership and audience figures that exist and the

variety of media from which to choose. The bad news is that as fragmentation of the media grows, such data must be taken with an increasingly large pinch of salt.

Television

Centralized media buying has brought costs down to advertisers in this area, but just what are they getting? Audience figures are unstable, and no-one is prepared to bet on when, if ever, they will settle down. Yet it offers the last of the 'mass' audiences and when used in conjunction with other communication channels can boost response rates. Bargains can also be had, since buying spots at less popular times of the day can guarantee specific, cheaper audiences. One fact worth bearing in mind is that the message may need repeating several times over, in different spots.

Pros
Glamour
Audience numbers
Ease of use

Cons
Production costs
Cost per target
Time on air
Limitations on message

Radio

A medium growing in popularity since the launch of franchises, offering the possibility of more selective regional audiences, therefore enhanced targeting. Costs are also competitive. Combined with sponsorships, it offers advertisers two bites at the cherry from a PR and a direct marketing point of view.

Pros
Enhanced targeting
Receptive audiences (keen on phone-ins)

Control (if you produce commercial yourself)
Competitive pricing

Cons
National coverage may be a problem
Lack of control (if you use station staff to do voice-over)

Print
New technology has raised the quality and accessibility of print media. It is possible to send copy and artwork down the line to newspapers, thereby reducing lead times and giving greater control over the finished product. Inaccuracies because of changes taken over the phone need no longer happen. New printing processes also offer advertisers greater flexibility of format, while rate cards are competitive.

Pros
International, national and regional availability
Socio-demographic breakdowns
Geodemographic breakdowns
Fast response
Colour facilities
Cost

Cons
Lack of quality control
Lack of distribution control

Consumer magazine pros
International, national and regional availability
Insert availability
Quality reproduction
Socio-demographic breakdowns
Geodemographic breakdowns
Long-term pulling power

Consumer magazine cons
Longer lead times than daily press
Cost

Trade magazine pros
As above, but tighter targeting

Trade magazine cons
As above

Inserts
This is a thriving area, especially when inserts are bound in to publications, enabling them to piggyback on a magazine's own brand value. It also has the advantage that, though possibly created for one magazine, you can commission run-ons for additional use in mailings, at point of sale, or in other publications. Inserts are also used in statement mailings.

Pros
Flexible format
Editorial and quality control
Cost
Adaptability
Ease of use for testing

Cons
Disposable (magazines held over bin to shake out
   inserts before reading)
Perceived as downmarket

Door-to-door
This is an area which, due to better demographic and socio-economic data, is growing in accuracy and effectiveness. It consists of the delivery of samples, items or advertising material direct to homes. It can work better on the Continent than in the UK, particularly in areas where the postal service leaves a lot to be desired.

Pros
Volume
Control over message and design

Cons
No control over recipient
Difficulty in high-rise areas, with large numbers of flats
Reliant on quality of deliverer
Can be expensive because of large numbers required

Telemarketing

This is a medium which has come of age, as the boundaries between outbound (calls made out for research and sales purposes) and inbound (responding to queries or purchase requests) start to blur. New software means that the same operators can be fed calls and scripts for both inbound and outbound, thus eliminating costly time wastage. It is, however, a medium which needs the personal touch as telephone teams require a good manager and motivator – quite apart from money. The team is your sales and service support staff. If you go outside to hire one, ensure that they are as professional as your own workforce.

Pros
Truly interactive
Effective
More personal
Immediate results
Can't be ignored
Measurable
Tailor made

Cons
Can be intrusive
Expensive
Labour intensive

INTERACTIVE MEDIA

Of all the media used for communicating with the customer, this is the most exciting. It does away with a lot of the restrictions which currently hamper marketing. Who wouldn't want to communicate with what they *know* is a sure-fire customer, in an instantaneous dialogue, which ensures that the *right* message is used?

For all the advance publicity, examples are still far from commonplace in the UK. The most likely to take off in the short term are those in showrooms, shopping malls, or airports. At some, travellers can approach a console, scan through an on-screen catalogue, and order their duty-frees by credit card to be delivered at home.

The development of multimedia, combining such disparate elements as telecommunications, computing and consumer electronics with media-like publishing, television and video, has given interactive added impetus. All it needs to overcome is the capital outlay needed to provide consumers with the means to communicate from home, and for the advertisers themselves to come to grips with the opportunities.

One of the possibilities is for consumers wishing to shop by catalogue from home, to be able to scan through an on-screen moving version. They will be able to call detail to the centre of the screen, and change the colours.

Interactive TV will force change on marketers. The medium will become an information/service provider and less sales input will be required. Since the customer will be paying per enquiry rather than per second, the message can be 15 minutes or longer if the product or service demands it.

LISTS
The limiting factor to many a campaign is the quality and availability of lists. You either go direct to the list owner, a list manager (who may keep these lists up to date) or to a broker who can advise on suitability and quality of available lists. Clients should aim for lists that are frequently cleaned and current.

Consumer lists

These range from mail order, questionnaire/lifestyle, and magazine lists to bookbuyers and cultural event attendees, with typical universes ranging from 40,000 to over 1 million. Geodemographic overlays such as Acorn, Mosaic and Superprofiles are available, and lifestyle databases can be rented from CMT, NDL and ICD.

Business-to-business lists

These are generally mail order buyers, seminar attendees, bookbuyers or magazine subscribers and universes range from 5,000 to 150,000 names. There are also subscriber/controlled circulation lists and compiled lists with selections such as job function, trade (SIC codes), size of company by employees or turnover, financial information, geographic and telephone numbers.

9

DESIGN

Its role in corporate identity and on supermarket shelves

WHAT IS DESIGN?

The role of good design is often underrated in the marketing mix. In the past, the best has often been taken for granted, the worst has provoked critical outbursts. The 1990s, however, has seen it gain recognition as a vital element in any purchasing decision, right up there with price, promotion and availability.

It also has a contribution to make to the public's perception of the company as a whole. In many cases, the brand is the corporate messenger, its only point of contact with customers. If the design, or indeed any element of the mix, alienates them, this will impact on how they see the corporate whole.

WHAT AREAS DOES IT COVER?

Design touches on every area of company business, but the most commonly quoted are:

> Graphics
> Interior
> Packaging
> Product
> NPD/Product extension
> Corporate
> Industrial

DESIGN'S IMPACT

Since food is no longer weighed up in individual portions in stores, as part of a personalized transaction, its packaging and advertising has a major role to play in the design–making process. This is true in virtually all areas of retail, and the pack needs to tie in with any support activity above or below the line.

In those sectors where the product is more amorphous, such as financial services, it is just as vital. All the high street banks have chosen to upgrade their premises, as have the building societies, to achieve differentiation and provide better customer service.

Even the treatment of a company's name, graphically, can reinforce brand qualities in the customer's mind. The Marks & Spencer logo recalls quality and reliability, McDonald's that of product and service uniformity.

In all areas, the benefits of design are measurable, both in terms of awareness and sales, when monitoring the results of changes by using a control. New product development can also be researched and test marketed.

WHY COMMISSION NEW DESIGN?

'If it ain't broke, don't fix it' goes the old maxim, but when sales are declining, sometimes it's hard to pinpoint whether design is at fault or whether it's just that the rest of the market has caught up.

If in doubt, the best solution is to commission research, both qualitative and quantitative. The main reasons for change, not necessarily valid ones, are the following: change of ownership, strategy switch, outdated design, sales figures, production advances, globalization, environmental, desire for corporate homogeneity, or just a design consultancy with a good chat-up line.

COMMISSIONING A DESIGN CONSULTANCY

If you do not possess an in-house design team, or require additional expertise, it's time to check out design consultants. Three points to bear in mind, if you want the best, are:

> check that they are specialists, instead of design being a fringe activity

> check that the principals are experienced in the design area you require
>
> beware of existing suppliers who claim they also 'do design'

Commissioning process

This is similar to that for commissioning specialists in other disciplines. The one aspect which sets it apart is that it is far more subjective than other areas, and very tempting for a client to overrule a consultancy on the grounds of personal likes or dislikes.

Prepare initial brief for consultancy which will cover the project, background data on the project, the market, the audience and the objectives. Give them any timing, production or budgetary limitations and an indication of how you expect work to be project managed.

Draw up a shortlist of consultancies, hopefully no more than three, having researched names through contacts or using industry information sources (see end of book). Meet to discuss methods of working, fees and view previous work. Ask for proposals in response to brief – and pay for work done.

After this, the process of commissioning and running a project will vary according to its nature. Let's look at the three main areas: corporate, product and packaging.

Corporate identity

This type of project will impact across everything your company does, so involve all communications advisers from the start. Also, create an internal team from all departments involved.

1. Background review

Consultant to study the company's strengths and weaknesses, internal and external perceptions, a visual audit of all items affected. It will also determine whether corporate strategy fits with existing corporate identity.

2. Brief development
When consultancy recommendations are taken on board, design brief proposals should be discussed.

3. Design concept generation
Concepts should be discussed and presented in a manner you are both comfortable with and which has been agreed beforehand. The consultancy should talk them through with you.

4. Mock-ups
A chance to see how concept needs will work across all items, such as stationery, livery, signs, etc.

5. Programme schedule
Client needs to work with consultancy to organize phased introduction of corporate identity, timed to coincide with any planned communications programme.

6. Launch
This needs to be approached as a two-way exercise, first internally to staff and then externally, possibly to the trade, and media, possibly the City and the public.

7. Execution
Post-launch, the consultancy has to go hell for leather to produce artwork and ensure faithfulness throughout to new identity.

8. Appraisal
This should measure changes compared with original research, to cover attitudes, media coverage, recall and cost efficiencies through rationalization.

Product design
A more focused process than corporate identity, tackling a new product for a new or existing market, or a

range extension. Alternatively it may involve modifications to an existing product.

1. Planning
Review your need for a full–service consultancy as against designs which can be executed in-house. Appoint project manager and team, and ensure consultancy has relevant experience. Scan contract carefully.

2. Brief development
Review brief with consultancy when appointed, taking account of corporate design and environmental policies, standards specifications and manufacturing capability.

3. Design concept generation
Consultancy to conduct its own research and produce ideas before finalizing brief with you. Initial thoughts are discussed with you before translation into first concepts. Client can then appreciate phased decision-making process.

5. Programme schedule
Process should assess production implications, alongside design of product itself. Final concepts are produced and tested, together with layout drawings to be viewed by in-house technical staff. The first model is presented, then refined, before detailed modelmaking plans are drawn up. A final model is presented.

6. Execution
The in-house team takes it back at this stage, although the consultant should monitor progress. The prototype is tested and reworked if necessary while the client should be tooled up ready for the launch.

7. Launch
Check marketing plans are set for launch, start pre-production runs, cross fingers, go.

8. Appraisal
Project team to evaluate all design stages and whether it has achieved objectives.

Packaging design
Design is a brand's main asset when competing with rivals on shelf including own brands. It can also communicate the brand owner's environmental credentials and sensitivity to national and cultural criteria.

1. Planning
Examine precise needs. It may be appropriate to ask for concepts only and examine ramifications before proceeding. The consultancy should display a knowledge of production processes and techniques, and strategic branding issues.

2. Brief development
Confirm why the project is being undertaken and its scope. Ensure the consultancy is given *all* relevant data.

3. Design concept generation
Consultancy research findings may challenge the brief. Once it is finalized, project schedule and costs may need reworking. First thoughts are translated in initial design concepts, which are then reviewed by project team and all in-house technical experts involved.

4. Programme schedule
When concept is finally chosen, and meets the brief, design will go through a phased development programme. It will be applied across range, with mock-ups which can be used for initial marketing or research. Designers to liaise with those who will produce finished version. Drawings signed off.

5. Execution

The consultant orders photography, finalizes text/graphics, contents list, health warnings and bar codes, and prepares production drawings. Artwork, when signed off, goes to the repro house, then proofed and printed. Check carefully.

6. Launch

If the designer has worked closely with a supplier or re-pro house, result should match design.

7. Appraisal

Research if design achieved objectives using control, and check attitudinal changes.

CREATIVITY

All marketers look for it, yet few really encourage it. Creativity, however, particularly in product planning, is key to success. Designers know that they can be presented with an earth-shattering piece of technology, but if they don't transform it into an appropriate product, one which consumers want to touch and use, it will be doomed to failure.

Look at the Sony Walkman. It has won award after award, and was seen as a design masterpiece of its time, yet it owes its success to creative marketing.

'Many have called the Walkman an innovative marvel, but where is the technology? Frankly, it did not contain any breakthrough technology. Its success was built on product planning and marketing.'
Akio Morito, Chairman of the Board, Sony Corporation, UK Innovation Lecture, 6 February 1992

Creativity is also required to protect brands, so that their identity can remain intact in the face of competition from own brands. This may be evident in an ultra-distinctive logo, or it may lie in the manufacturing process itself. A new container, or packaging, which has required the manufacturer to invest heavily in production plant, may give a brand a useful breathing space on shelf. Rivals would also need to expend time and money to produce anything similar.

NEW TECHNOLOGY

Of all the disciplines, new technology has had the main impact on the design sector. Data may be sent down the wire from one country to another in international market research, but in design the impact has been far more dramatic.

Where computers can be used more cheaply and more effectively, paper is on the way out. Less paperwork means designers can spend longer on the creative aspects of concept work, rather than cutting and pasting.

Clients relish the fact that they can see finished artwork on screen, and can experiment with different colours. Unfortunately, this can encourage a tendency to over-experiment, which can lead to costly delays.

New technology is being used ever earlier in the creative process, even resulting in design manuals being put on computer. It is at the production stage, however, that new technology can cut costs and raise quality, if designers feed printers either film or disc.

10

PUBLIC RELATIONS

*It can open doors to new markets and defuse crisis points.
Allied with sponsorship its potential is dynamite.*

Suppose you're a soft drinks manufacturer in the middle of a heatwave and a crank tries to blackmail you by spiking your product. Or a retailer wishing to build on a grass field site and coming up against opposition from the community. Or an ice-cream maker who thinks that advertising is a waste of money.

What do all these have in common? Yes, you've guessed it, the need for some good public relations.

DEFINITIONS

'Public Relations is about reputation – the result of what you do, what you say and what others say about you.

PR practice is the discipline which looks after reputation with the aim of earning understanding and support and influencing opinion and behaviour.'

Institute of Public Relations

The danger inherent in this definition is that it isolates public relations. In fact, any marketing programme is likely to have a PR component. Don't leave it out, just plan it properly. Think integrated marketing.

PLANNING
Planning is an established part of advertising. Planners fulfil a strategic role. They can translate what the client really wants, but can't always define, into a long-term marketing programme. In press relations, the role of planning is not so clear cut.

In the past, consultants have helped promote news or

views that a client wants broadcast. This was relatively simple in a country with only so much print media, few TV and radio channels and rigid laws governing sponsorship and advertising.

In the 1990s, however, the media explosion and looser sponsorship guidelines mean coverage can no longer be measured in column inches – if it ever could – and more planning needs to take place to target PR messages. As in any promotional activity, three points need to be borne in mind:

> isolate who you wish to talk to, or the different types of people you are interested in
> determine the message(s) you wish to send each one
> work out which is the most appropriate vehicle for each one

COMMUNICATION

The above deals with media as defined by press and broadcast, but the beauty of PR is that it transcends these borders. Again, it depends on the message and the audience, but the appropriate vehicle could be:

> An event/exhibition
> A newsletter
> An award
> Community involvement
> Internal PR
> Education/Charity/Environmental schemes

WHY PR?

Probably a better question is why not? Since any form of marketing involves change, PR has a pro–active role in reinforcing it and a reactive, sometimes a defensive, role in dealing with changes. It can also prove a great deal less expensive than advertising, yet just as effective for some brands, always a convincing argument for marketers.

Product PR

Take Jacob's Bakery. It brought out a 'dinosaurs biscuit' for children but did not have the budget for a big ad or sales promotion campaign. Public relations came to the rescue. In conjunction with its consultancy, Handel Communications, Jacob's identified its audience, parents and children, and the media needed to reach them. A range of communication messages was devised to promote trial and reinforce branding. The campaign's main elements were:

Child activity pack, endorsed by Natural History Museum
Colouring competition
Dinosaur play-bus which toured city centres
Money-off vouchers

Results: sales 100 per cent above target, total potential audience reach of over 59 million, and sparked an ongoing education-based campaign.

Defensive PR

A company's worst nightmare is to have one of its brands nobbled, and even the best-known brands are vulnerable. Heinz fell prey to a blackmailer who put broken up razor blades into jars of its baby foods. Its cans were untouched. (For some reason, history has it that the perpetrator used broken glass, but this was used in copycat crimes only.) Knowing the damage that could be caused to its customers and its reputation, the company set in place an immediate action plan.

It advertised a series of hotlines which the public could ring for reassurance about which jars had been affected

Spokesmen went on air at prime time to allay fears

It took the jars off shelf, replacing them as soon as possible while advising consumers how to check for tampering. Glass jars already had pop up tops, so intrusion was fairly easy to detect. Also, if jar had been unsealed and put back on shelf for any length of time, it would smell 'off' when top was removed again.

Four weeks after the crisis went public, Heinz had introduced tamper-evident sleeving to its products. This was seen as the best way of alleviating public concern. It communicated this step via public announcements, then by taking ads in publications or sections of publications aimed at mothers with young children, and then by direct mail. This was its first use of direct mail, ironic given its recent decision to focus on this communication medium.

Results: The company emerged with its reputation enhanced, if anything, as a caring company, and the development of tamper proof jars and seals was a giant step forward.

It does not, however, always work this smoothly. If a company does not have a crisis-management programme worked out, it is at the mercy of the elements. Spokesmen look shaken because they haven't been able to work out a script in time, emergency phone lines are delayed, the overwhelming impression is one of confusion. The company loses respect and sales, and can take years to recover. Yet all this is avoidable.

Corporate PR
A company may have inherited a reputation which no longer bears any relevance to its current situation. If a corporate strategy is not devised to reposition it, no

amount of chipping away at its status will do any good. This proved the case with a national UK carpet and furnishings manufacturer and retailer, who shall remain nameless.

It briefed Countrywide Communications Limited, one of Britain's top five consultancies, to instigate a communications programme that would help change its reputation. It wanted to be seen as a home furnishings specialist, not simply a 'pile-it-high' carpet retailer.

The highlight of the vast media relations programme undertaken was a national interior design competition, sponsored by the retailer, involving design students, professional designers and customers and endorsed by the Design Council. The competition applauded creativity, using easily available furnishings, demonstrating that style was readily achievable using the choice of goods at this high street retailer.

Managing PR
Effective PR management depends on the client's understanding of what it can achieve, how to agree a brief and set objectives. If a company is new, PR tends to be lumped in with the marketing function, since product launches will inevitably need publicity. Corporate PR may be neglected, an oversight companies often come to regret.

One for all?
A small firm in need of PR faces a simple choice: whether to handle it in-house or appoint a consultancy. Opting for in-house means more control over your message, and possibly cost savings, but more legwork in organizing press coverage, more creativity in arranging events. An expert might prove more cost-effective.

For a bigger company, the choice is more complicated.

The strategy makers will stay in-house, but should you opt for one consultancy big enough to handle all its brands or several, possibly specialist, agencies?

In either case, it is advisable to spend time thinking about what you want out of PR, now and in the future, and then to assess corporate strengths and weaknesses against those objectives, before appointing a consultant. It's a two-way process; clients must be professional about communicating needs and ideas to the consultancy, and giving them information when they need it.

Big-name consultancy pros

Longevity may indicate it's recession proof
May provide a more co-ordinated approach
Agency 'champions' brand and company
May have more initial clout with media

Big-name consultancy cons

Tough sustaining creative impetus
Hard to maintain competitiveness of rival brands
May have high overheads, therefore cost more
If agency underperforms, you have a problem
    across the whole company and range of
    products
High staff turnover

Specialist consultancy pros

Specialist expertise
Undivided attention
Avoids conflict between different parts of same
    organization
If agency underperforms, at least the problem is
    limited to one part of the organization

Specialist consultancy cons

Needs more co-ordinating
May compete between each other for client time
May have less media penetration

SPONSORSHIP
Sponsorship is a no-man's land. The advertising and PR industries lay claim to it, yet though the tasks it performs relate to both its potential is greater than either.

What is it?
Any definition is limited by the fact that the sponsorship industry is changing so fast. Whereas a decade ago it was associated mainly with events, nowadays the main growth area is broadcast sponsorship, with a myriad of opportunities in between.

The classic explanation is that sponsorship is an association between an event and rights owner where certain benefits of association are granted for a consideration of either cash or services. Yet it is much more: it is also a communications medium, one which incorporates all the marketing disciplines.

Benefits
If a company is interested in any of the following, sponsorship can help. It can:

create awareness
change attitudes
create sampling opportunities
boost sales
incentivize salesforce
build loyalty with suppliers
create goodwill
offer advertising opportunities
cost-effective targeting
offer corporate hospitality

The reason why it is one of the most exciting media, though, is the way it works in harness with, say, sales promotion, direct marketing, advertising and PR. When used properly, it personifies integrated marketing.

Versatility

It is hard to find an area in which sponsorship *cannot* work. Take education. The co-op, when it decided it wanted to heighten name awareness among young people and their families and boost its community-oriented profile, sought out an area of the national curriculum which matched its objectives. It picked a topic called Personal and Social Education (PSE), bringing out a sponsored handbook to help teachers, linked with a competition, and transforming winning entries into TV shorts.

In retail, by contrast, it's easy to operate countrywide tours, visiting shopping malls and offering make-overs to customers while running sponsored fashion shows. In one swoop, a client can raise awareness, create sampling opportunities, build loyalty and, if it chooses to televise the process, create a commercial.

Pioneering

Household products have been major users of sponsorship in the US for a while, but in this country Lever Bros. has been the first to do more than dip its toe in the water. In May 1993 it launched a three-year initiative called Persil Funfit with a budget estimated at between £3m and £4m.

It offers participants:

a teacher's National Curriculum Resource Pack

a special pack of pre-school playgroup leaders

a reward scheme with a series of certificates and badges for each age group linked to performance in a range of fitness-based activities

a collector programme for free games equipment

The scheme will stand the test of time because not only has it proved successful so far (prompting awareness of 47 per cent, beating its 30 per cent target) but because its objectives were so well researched. They included:

a detailed brief, defining the brand's requirements for major activity that involved its core market, housewives with children, and reinforcing its caring image in an innovative and contemporary manner

a potential long-term commitment to a programme that proved its effectiveness

research to be built in at all stages of the programme

extensive concept testing prior to the announcement of the sponsorship

the use of two sponsorship consultancies: one to co-ordinate and develop Funfit itself, APA, and the other to monitor the performance of the main agency, Karen Earl

Lever is likely to build on a successful first year and innovate its way into the second. It is even examining the merits of broadcast sponsorship.

Broadcast sponsorship

This fast-growing area offers sponsors a wide range of benefits if they should choose to exploit them. There are three dangers: one is that a client is persuaded to add his brand's name to a programme which is an exact match, another is when a successful partnership between sponsor and sponsored is ruined through both trying to drive too hard a bargain, and the final one is when a client fails to fund the promotion of its involvement.

In all sponsorship, it's tempting to think that the upfront spend should be sufficient investment. Yet depending on the client's objectives, it could incorporate on-pack promotions tied to a sponsored programme, local press competitions, community events, educational tie-ins – the opportunities are endless.

Measurement
As with any other communications medium, the problems start with measuring effectiveness, so objectives need to incorporate a device to isolate the performance of sponsorship against the other items in the mix. Sometimes this is impossible, yet nine times out of ten it is achievable.

11

SELECTION OF TRADE ORGANIZATIONS, ASSOCIATIONS AND INSTITUTES

Advertising Association
Abford House
15 Wilton Road
London
SW1V 1NJ
0171 828 2771

Advertising Standards Authority
Brook House
2–16 Torrington Place
London
WC1E 7HN
0171 580 5555

Association of Marketing Survey Organizations
89 Church Lane
London
N2 0TH
0181 444 3692

Broadcasters' Audience Research Board
Glenthorne House
Hammersmith Grove
London
W6 0ND
0181 741 9110

Broadcasting Standards Council
5/8 The Sanctuary
London
SW1P 3JS
0171 233 0544

British Institute of Management
Management House
Cottingham Road
NN17 1TT
0536 204222

Chartered Institute of Marketing
Moor Hall
Cookham
Maidenhead
Berkshire
SL6 9QH
06285 24922

Communication, Advertising and Marketing
    Foundation (CAM) Ltd
Abford House
15 Wilton Road
London
SW1V 1NG
0171 828 7506

Confederation of British Industry (CBI)
Centre Point
103 New Oxford Street
London
WC1A 1DU
0171 379 7400

Data Protection Registrar
Wycliffe House
Water Lane
Wilmslow
Cheshire
SK9 5AY
0625 535777

Design Business Association (DBA)
and Chartered Society of Designers
29 Bedford Square
London
WC1B 3EG
0171 631 1510

Direct Marketing Association
Haymarket House
1 Oxendon Street
London
SW1Y 4EE
0171 321 2525

Direct Mail Services Standards Board (DMSS)
26 Eccleston Street
London
SW1W 9PY
0171 824 8651

European Sponsorship Consultants Association
c/o Helen Day Promotions
34 Hill Street
Richmond
Surrey
TW9 1TW
0181 332 9889

Incorporated Society of British Advertisers
44 Hertford Street
London
W1Y 8AE
0171 499 7502

Independent Television Commission
33 Foley Street
London
W1P 7LP
0171 255 3000

Institute of Directors
116 Pall Mall
London
SW1Y 5ED
0171 839 1233

Institute of Direct Marketing
No. 1 Park Road
Teddington
Middlesex
TW11 0AR
0181 977 5705

The Institute of Packaging
Sysonby Lodge
Nottingham Road
Melton Mowbray
Leics. LE13 6NU
06645 00055

Institute of Practitioners in Advertising (IPA)
44, Belgrave Square
London
SW1X 8QS
0171 235 7020

Institute of Public Relations
The Old Trading House
15 Northburgh Street
London
EC1V 0PR
0171 253 5151

Institute of Sales Promotion (ISP and SPCA)
Arena House
66–68 Pentonville Road
London
N1 9HS
0171 837 5340

Mailing Preference Service
No. 5 Rees House
Plantation Wharf
London
SW10 3UF
0171 738 1625

Market Research Society (MRS)
15 Northburgh Street
London
EC1V 0AH
0171 490 4911

The Marketing Society
St George's House
3–5 Pepys Road
SW20 8NJ
0181 879 3464

The Newspaper Society
Bloomsbury House
74/77 Great Russell Street
London
WC1B 3DA
0171 636 7014

Public Relations Consultants Association
Willow House
Willow Place
Victoria
London
SW1P 1JH
0171 233 6026